Sanctum Rosariu~

Let us put ourselves in the presence of God

Per signum (†) Sancte Crucis, de inimicis (†) nostris libera nos, Domine (†) Deus noster.

By the sign (†) of the Holy Cross, deliver us (†) from our enemies, O Lord (†) our God.

In nomine Patris (†), et Filii, et Spiritus Sancti. Amen.

In the name of the Father (†), and of the Son, and of the Holy Spirit. Amen.

Prayer to the Holy Spirit

Veni, Sancte Spíritus!, reple tuórum corda fidélium: et tui amóris in eis ignem accénde.

Come, Holy Spirit! Fill the hearts of your faithful and kindle in them the fire of your love.

V. Emitte Spíritum tuum, et creabúntur.

V. Send forth your Spirit and they shall be created.

R. Et renovábis faciem terræ.

R. And you shall renew the face of the earth.

Deus, qui corda fidélium Sancti Spíritus illustratióne docuísti, da nobis in eódem Spíritu recta sápere; et de eius semper consolatióne gaudére. Per Christum Dóminum nostrum. Amen.

O God, who by the light of the Holy Spirit, did instruct the hearts of the faithful, grant that by the same Holy Spirit we may be truly wise and ever enjoy His consolations. Through Christ Our Lord. Amen.

Let us pray

V. Domine, labia mea aperies.

V. Lord, open my lips.

R. Et os meum annuntiabit laudem tuam.

R. And my mouth will proclaim your praise.

V. Deus, in adiutórium meum intende.

V. O God, come to my assistance.

R. Dómine, ad adiuvándum me festina.

R. O Lord, make haste to help me.

V. Gloria Patri, et Filio, et Spiritui Sancto.

V. Glory be to the Father, and to the Son, and to the Holy Spirit.

R. Sicut erat in princípio et nunc et semper, et in sæcula sæculorum. Amen.

R. As it was in the beginning, is now, and ever shall be, world without end. Amen.

V. Dignare me laudare Te, Virgo Sacrata.

V. Allow me to praise You, O sacred Virgin.

R. Da mihi virtutem contra hostes tuos.

R. Give me strength against your enemies.

Act of contrition

O mi Dómine Iesu, verus Deus et Homo verus, Creátor, Pater et Redémptor meus, in qui credo et spero, et quem super ómnia díligo: Me poénitet ex toto corde propter peccáta mea,

Lord Jesus Christ, true God and man, my Creator, Father and Redeemer, in whom I believe and hope. I love you above all else, and I am sorry with all my heart for my sins.

quia Tu Deus bonus es, ac me poenis inférni puníre potes et Tua gratia adiuvánte emendatiónem in futúris pollíceor. Amen.

You are the Supreme Good, and I may deserve the pains of hell. I firmly intend with your grace, to do penance, and to avoid whatever leads me to sin, to never to offend you again. Amen.

Offering of the Holy Rosary

Domine Deus noster, dirige et educ omnes nostras cogitationes, verba, affectus, opera et desideria ad maiorem Tuum honorem et gloriam.

Direct, O Lord, we beseech you, all our actions by your holy inspirations, and carry them on by your gracious assistance, that every thought, word, and deed of ours may begin always from you, and by you be happily ended.

Et Te, Virgo beatissima, a Filio Tuo largire ut attente ac devote hanc coronam Sanctissimi Tui Rosarii recitemus, quam pro Sanctae Matris Ecclesiae atque nostris necessitatibus tam spiritualibus quam temporalibus offerimus, necnon et pro bono vivorum et suffragio defunctorum gratulationis Tuae ac maioris nostrae obligationis.

And You, O Most Holy Virgin, through your Son, we implore you, inspire in our hearts a fervent love for the recitation of the Rosary. We offer it for Holy Mother Church, our spiritual and temporal needs, as well as the good of the living and the suffrages for the dead, which are pleasing to you and our greatest duty.

*We offer it especially for... **particular intention.***

Apostles' Creed

Credo in Deum, Patrem omnipoténtem, Creatórem cæli et terræ.

I believe in God, the Father almighty, Creator of heaven and earth.

Et in Iesum Christum, Fílium eius únicum, Dóminum nostrum: qui concéptus est de Spíritu Sancto, natus ex María Vírgine, passus sub Póntio Piláto, crucifíxus, mórtuus, et sepúltus, descéndit ad ínferos; tértia die resurréxit a mórtuis; ascéndit ad cælos; sedet ad déxteram Dei Patris omnipoténtis: inde ventúrus est iudicáre vivos et mórtuos.

And in Jesus Christ, His only Son, our Lord, Who was conceived by the Holy Spirit, born of the Virgin Mary, suffered under Pontius Pilate, was crucified, died and was buried, He descended into hell. On the third day He rose again from the dead; He ascended into heaven, and is seated at the right hand of God the Father almighty; from there he will come to judge the living and the dead.

Credo in Spíritum Sanctum, Sanctam Ecclésiam Cathólicam, Sanctórum communiónem, remissiónem peccatórum, carnis resurrectiónem, vitam ætérnam. Amen.

I believe in the Holy Spirit, the Holy Catholic Church, the communion of saints, the forgiveness of sins, the resurrection of the body, and life everlasting. Amen.

How to pray?

*Pray the **Our Father**, three **Hail Marys** y the **Glory be**.*

*Announce the first Mistery, pause to meditate on it, and pray the **Our Father**, ten **Hail Marys**, the **Glory be**, and the **Brief prayers**.*

Now repeat, announce a new Mystery, with its respective prayers.

Pater Noster, qui es in cælis, sanctificétur nomen Tuum, adveniat Regnum Tuum, fiat volúntas tua, sicut in cælo et in terra.

Our Father, who art in heaven, hallowed be thy name; thy kingdom come; thy will be done on earth as it is in heaven.

R. Panem nostrum quotidiánum da nobis hódie, et dimitte nobis débita nostra, sicut et nos dimíttimus debitóribus nostris; et ne nos indúcas in tentationem, sed libera nos a malo. Amen.

R. Give us this day our daily bread; and forgive us our trespasses as we forgive those who trespass against us; and lead us not into temptation, but deliver us from evil. Amen.

Hail Mary

Ave Maria, gratia plena, Dominus tecum, benedicta tu in muliéribus, et benedictus fructus ventris tui Iesus.

Hail, Mary, full of grace, the Lord is with thee. Blessed art thou amongst women and blessed is the fruit of thy womb, Jesus.

R. Sancta Maria, Mater Dei, ora pro nobis peccatoribus, nunc et in hora mortis nostræ. Amen.

R. Holy Mary, Mother of God, pray for us sinners, now and at the hour of our death. Amen.

Glory Be

V. Gloria Patri, et Filio, et Spiritui Sancto.

V. Glory be to the Father, to the Son, and to the Holy Spirit.

R. Sicut erat in princípio et nunc et semper, et in sæcula sæculorum. Amen.

R. As it was in the beginning, is now, and ever shall be, world without end. Amen.

*On Good Friday, instead of the **Glory Be**, you can pray:*

V. Christus factus est pro nobis obœdiens usque ad mortem.

V. Christ became obedient for us unto death.

R. Mortem autem crucis.

R. Even to death on a cross.

And on Holy Saturday:

V. Christus factus est pro nobis obœdiens usque ad mortem, mortem autem crucis.

V. Christ became obedient for us unto death, even to death on a cross.

R. Propter quod et Deus exaltávit íllum: et dedit ílli nomen, quod est super omne nomen.

R. Because of this, God greatly exalted him and bestowed on him the name that is above every name.

Brief Prayers

V. Maria Mater gratiæ, Mater misericordiæ.

V. Mary, Mother of grace, Mother of mercy.

R. Tu nos ab hoste protege et hora mortis suscipe.

R. Protect us from the enemy and receive us at the hour of death.

O mi Iesu, dimitte nobis débita nostra, salvanos ab igne infernis, perduc in cælum omnes ánimas præsértim eas quæ misericórdiæ tuæ máxime índigent. Amen.

O my Jesus, forgive us our sins and save us from the fires of hell. Lead all souls to heaven, especially those in most need of Thy mercy. Amen.

Presentation of Christ in the Temple
Philippe de Champaigne (1602-1674)

Mysteria Gaudiosa

(in feria secunda et in sabbato)

The Joyful Mysteries

(Monday and Saturday)

Primum Mysterium: Beatæ Mariæ Virginis anuntiatiónem contemplámur, et humílitas pétitur.

First Mystery: We contemplate the Annunciation of the Blessed Virgin Mary and we ask for humility.

Secundum Mysterium: Beatæ Mariæ Virginis visitatiónem contemplámur, et charitas ad fratres pétitur.

Second Mystery: We contemplate the visitation of the Blessed Virgin Mary to St. Elizabeth and we ask for love of neighbor.

Tertium Mysterium: Domini Nostri Iesu Christi nativitátem contemplámur, et paupertátis spíritus pétitur.

Third Mystery: We contemplate the Birth of Our Lord Jesus Christ and we ask for love of poverty.

Quartum Mysterium: Domini Nostri Iesu Christi presentatiónem in templo contemplámur, et obediéntia pétitur.

Fourth Mystery: We contemplate the Presentation of the Child Jesus in the Temple and we ask for obedience.

Quintum Mysterium: Domini Nostri Iesu Christi inventiónem in templo contemplámur, et Deum inquæréndi volúntas pétitur.

Fifth Mystery: We contemplate The Finding of the Child Jesus in the Temple and we ask for desire to seek God.

Triptych: The Crucifixion
Rogier van der Weyden (1399-1464)

Mysteria Dolorosa

(in feria tertia et in feria sexta)

The Sorrowful Mysteries

(Tuesday and Friday)

Primum Mysterium: Domini Nostri Iesu Christi oratiónem in horto contemplámur, et dólor pro peccatis nostris pétitur.

First Mystery: We contemplate the Prayer and Agony of Our Lord Jesus Christ in the Garden and we ask for contrition of our sins.

Secundum Mysterium: Domini Nostri Iesu Christi flagellatiónem contemplámur, et córporum nostrórum mortificátio pétitur.

Second Mystery: We contemplate the Scourging of Our Lord Jesus Christ and we ask for mortification of the flesh.

Tertium Mysterium: Domini Nostri Iesu Christi spinis coronationem contemplámur, et supérbiæ mortificatio pétitur.

Third Mystery: We contemplate the Crowning of Our Lord Jesus Christ with Thorns and we ask for mortification of pride.

Quartum Mysterium: Domini Nostri Iesu Christi crucis baiulatiónem contemplámur, et patiéntia in tribulatiónibus pétitur.

Fourth Mystery: We contemplate the Carrying of the Cross and we ask for patience in tribulation.

Quintum Mysterium: Domini Nostri Iesu Christi crucifixiónem et mortem contemplámur, et súi ipsíus donum ad animárum redemptiónem pétitur.

Fifth Mystery: We contemplate the Crucifixion and Death of Our Lord Jesus Christ and we ask for love of God and the salvation of souls.

The Pentecost
Fray Juan Bautista Maino (1581-1649)

Mysteria Gloriosa

(in die Dominico et in feria quarta)

The Glorious Mysteries

(Sunday & Wednesday)

Primum Mysterium: Domini Nostri Iesu Christi resurrectiónem contemplamur, et fídes pétitur.

First Mystery: We contemplate the Resurrection of Our Lord Jesus Christ from the Dead and we ask for faith.

Secundum Mysterium: Domini Nostri Iesu Christi in cælum ascensiónem contemplamur, et spes pétitur.

Second Mystery: We contemplate the Ascension of Our Lord Jesus Christ into Heaven and we ask for hope and the desire for heaven.

Tertium Mysterium: Spiritus Sancti descensiónem contemplamur, et cháritas ad Deum pétitur.

Third Mystery: We contemplate the Descent of the Holy Spirit on the Apostles and we ask for charity.

Quartum Mysterium: Beatæ Mariæ Virginis in cælum assumptiónem contemplamur, et bene moriéndi gratia pétitur.

Fourth Mystery: We contemplate the Assumption of the Blessed Virgin Mary into Heaven and we ask for the grace of a happy death.

Quintum Mysterium: Beatæ Mariæ Virginis coronatiónem contemplamur, et fidúcia in María Regína Nostra pétitur.

Fifth Mystery: We contemplate the Coronation of the Blessed Virgin Mary in Heaven and we ask for trust in Mary.

The Marriage Feast at Cana
Bartolome Esteban Murillo (1617-1682)

Mysteria Luminosa

(in feria quinta)

The Luminous Mysteries

(Thursday)

Primum mysterium: Domini Nostri Iesu Christi in Iordáne baptizátur.

First Mystery: The Baptism of Our Lord Jesus Christ in the River Jordan.

Secundum mysterium: Domini Nostri Iesu Christi apud Canénse Matrimónium se autorevélat.

Second Mystery: Our Lord Jesus Christ revealing himself in the Wedding Feast at Cana.

Tertium mysterium: Domini Nostri Iesu Christi regnum Dei proclámat et ad conversiónem invítat.

Third Mystery: Our Lord Jesus Christ proclaiming the Coming of the Kingdom of God and the call to conversion.

Quartum mysterium: Domini Nostri Iesu Christi in monte Thabor transfigurátur.

Fourth Mystery: The transfiguration of Our Lord Jesus Christ on Mount Tabor.

Quintum mysterium: Domini Nostri Iesu Christi Eucharístiam instítuit.

Fifth Mystery: Our Lord Jesus Christ institutes the Eucharist.

*Once the Mysteries are completed, pray the **Our Father,** and then the following prayers:*

Ave Maria Sanctíssima, Dei Patris Filia, Virgo purissima ante partum, in manus tuas commendo fidem meam illuminandam. Gratia plena, Dominus tecum, benedicta tu in muliéribus, et benedictus fructus ventris tui Iesus.

Hail Mary, Daughter of God the Father, Virgin most pure before childbirth, into your hands we entrust our faith so that you may enlighten it. Full of grace, the Lord is with thee. Blessed art thou amongst women and blessed is the fruit of thy womb, Jesus.

R. Sancta Maria, Mater Dei, ora pro nobis peccatoribus, nunc et in hora mortis nostræ. Amen.

R. Holy Mary, Mother of God, pray for us sinners, now and at the hour of our death. Amen.

Ave Maria Sanctíssima, Dei Filii Mater, Virgo purissima in partum, in manus tuas commendo spem meam erigendam. Gratia plena, Dominus tecum, benedicta tu in muliéribus, et benedictus fructus ventris tui Iesus.

Hail Mary, Mother of God the Son, Virgin most pure during childbirth, into your hands we entrust our hope so that you may encourage it. Full of grace, the Lord is with thee. Blessed art thou amongst women and blessed is the fruit of thy womb, Jesus.

R. Sancta Maria, Mater Dei, ora pro nobis peccatoribus, nunc et in hora mortis nostræ. Amen.

R. Holy Mary, Mother of God, pray for us sinners, now and at the hour of our death. Amen.

Ave Maria Sanctíssima, Dei Spiritus Sancti Sponsa, Virgo purissima post partum, in manus tuas commendo caritate meam inflamandam. Gratia plena, Dominus tecum, benedicta tu in muliéribus, et benedictus fructus ventris tui Iesus.

R. Sancta Maria, Mater Dei, ora pro nobis peccatoribus, nunc et in hora mortis nostræ. Amen.

Hail Mary, Spouse of God the Holy Spirit, Virgin most pure after childbirth, into your hands we entrust our charity so that you may kindle it. Full of grace, the Lord is with thee. Blessed art thou amongst women and blessed is the fruit of thy womb, Jesus.

R. Holy Mary, Mother of God, pray for us sinners, now and at the hour of our death. Amen.

Ave Maria Sanctíssima, Templum et Sacrarium Sanctissimæ et Augustissimæ Trinitatis, Virgo purissima sine labe originali concepta.

Hail Mary, Temple and Sanctuary of the Most Holy Trinity, Virgin most pure conceived without original sin.

R. Sálve, Regína, Máter misericórdiæ, vita, dulcédo, et spes nóstra, sálve. Ad te clamámus, éxsules fílii Hevæ. Ad te suspirámus, geméntes et fléntes, in hac lacrimárum valle.

R. Hail, Holy Queen, Mother of mercy, our life, our sweetness, and our hope! To thee do we cry, poor banished children of Eve. To thee do we send up our sighs, mourning and weeping in this valley of tears.

Eia, ergo, advocáta nóstra, illos túos misericórdes óculos ad nos convérte.

Turn then, most gracious advocate, thine eyes of mercy toward us.

Et Iésum, benedíctum frúctum véntris tui, nobis post hoc exilium osténde. O clémens, O pía, O dúlcis Vírgo María.

And after this our exile, show unto us the blessed fruit of thy womb, Jesus. O clement, O loving, O sweet Virgin Mary!

V. Ora pro nobis, Sancta Dei Genetrix.

V. Pray for us, O Holy Mother of God.

R. Ut digni efficiamur promissionibus Christi.

R. That we may be made worthy of the promises of Christ.

Litany of the Blessed Virgin Mary

V. Kyrie, eleison.

V. Lord, have mercy on us.

R. Kyrie, eleison.

R. Lord, have mercy on us.

V. Christe, eleison.

V. Christ, have mercy on us.

R. Christe, eleison.

R. Christ, have mercy on us.

V. Kyrie, eleison.	V. Lord, have mercy on us.
R. Kyrie, eleison.	R. Lord, have mercy on us.
V. Christe, audi nos.	V. Christ hear us.
R. Christe, audi nos.	R. Christ hear us.
V. Christe, exaudi nos.	V. Christ, graciously hear us.
R. Christe, exaudi nos.	R. Christ, graciously hear us.
V. Pater de cælis Deus.	V. God the Father of heaven.
R. Miserere nobis.	R. Have mercy on us.
V. Fili Redemptor mundi Deus.	V. God the Son, Redeemer of the world.
R. Miserere nobis.	R. Have mercy on us.
V. Spiritus Sancte Deus.	V. God the Holy Spirit.
R. Miserere nobis.	R. Have mercy on us.
V. Sancta Trinitas, unus Deus.	V. Holy Trinity, one God.
R. Miserere nobis.	R. Have mercy on us.

Sancta María,	Holy Mary,
ora pro nobis...	*pray for us…*
Sancta Dei Génetrix	Holy Mother of God
Sancta Virgo vírginum	Holy Virgin of virgins
Mater Christi	Mother of Christ
Mater Ecclesiae	Mother of the Church
Mater Misericordiæ	Mother of Mercy
Mater divínæ grátiæ	Mother of divine grace
Mater Spei	Mother of Hope
Mater puríssima	Mother most pure
Mater castíssima	Mother most chaste
Mater invioláta	Mother inviolate
Mater intemeráta	Mother undefiled
Mater amábilis	Mother most amiable
Mater admirábilis	Mother admirable
Mater Boni Consílii	Mother of Good Counsel
Mater Creatóris	Mother of our Creator
Mater Salvatóris	Mother of our Saviour
Virgo prudentíssima	Virgin most prudent
Virgo veneránda	Virgin most venerable
Virgo prædicánda	Virgin most renowned
Virgo potens	Virgin most powerful
Virgo clemens	Virgin most merciful
Virgo fidélis	Virgin most faithful

Spéculum iustítiæ	Mirror of justice
Sedes sapiéntiæ	Seat of wisdom
Causa nostræ laetítiæ	Cause of our joy
Vas spirituále	Spiritual vessel
Vas honorábile	Vessel of honour
Vas insígne devotiónis	Singular vessel of devotion
Rosa mystica	Mystical rose
Turris Davídica	Tower of David
Turris ebúrnea	Tower if ivory
Domus áurea	House of gold
Foéderis arca	Ark of the covenant
Iánua cæli	Gate of heaven
Stella matutína	Morning star
Salus infirmórum	Health of the sick
Refúgium peccatórum	Refuge of sinners
Solacium migrantium	Solace of Migrants
Consolátrix afflictórum	Comfort of the afflicted
Auxílium Christianórum	Help of Christians
Regína Angelórum	Queen of Angels,
Regína Patriarchárum	Queen of Patriarchs

Regína Prophetárum	Queen of Prophets
Regína Apostolórum	Queen of Apostles
Regína Mártyrum	Queen of Martyrs
Regína Confessórum	Queen of Confessors
Regína Vírginum	Queen of Virgins
Regína Sanctórum ómnium	Queen of all Saints
Regína sine labe originali concépta	Queen conceived without original sin
Regína in cælum assúmpta	Queen assumed into heaven
Regína Sacratíssimi Rosárii	Queen of the most holy Rosary
Regina familiæ	Queen of families
Regína pacis	Queen of peace.

V. Agnus Dei, qui tollis peccata mundi.	V. Lamb of God, who takes away the sins of the world.
R. Parce nobis, Domine.	R. Spare us, O Lord.
V. Agnus Dei, qui tollis peccata mundi.	V. Lamb of God, who takes away the sins of the world.
R. Exaudi nos, Domine.	R. Graciously hear us, O Lord

V. Agnus Dei, qui tollis peccata mundi.

R. Miserere nobis.

V. Lamb of God, who takes away the sins of the world.

R. Have mercy on us.

Deus cuius Unigénitus per vitam, mortem et resurrectiónem suam nobis salútis ætérnæ præmia comparávit: concéde, quæsumus; ut, hæc mystéria sacratíssimo beátæ Maríæ Virginis Rosário recolentes, et imitémur quod cóntinent, et quod promíttunt, assequámur. Per eúmdem Christum Dóminum nostrum. Amen.

O God, whose only-begotten Son, by His life, death, and resurrection, has purchased for us the rewards of eternal salvation; grant we beseech Thee, that meditating upon these mysteries of the most holy Rosary of the Blessed Virgin Mary, we may imitate what they contain and obtain what they promise. Through Christ our Lord. Amen.

Closing prayers

Concede nos, fámulos tuos quǽsumus Dómine Deus, perpetua mentis et córporis sanitáte gaudére, et gloriósa beatæ Maríæ semper Vírginis intercessione, a præsenti liberári tristitia, et æterna pérfrui lætitia. Per Christum Dóminum nostrum. Amen.

Grant, we beseech Thee, O Lord God, that we Thy Servants may enjoy perpetual health of mind and body; and by the glorious intercession of the Blessed Mary, ever Virgin, be delivered from present sorrow, and obtain eternal joy. Through Christ Our Lord. Amen.

Sub tuum præsidium confugimus, Sancta Dei Genetrix: nostras deprecationes ne despicias in necesitatibus, sed a periculis cunctis libera nos semper, Virgo gloriosa et Benedicta.

We fly to Thy protection, O Holy Mother of God. Do not despise our petitions in our necessities, but deliver us always from all dangers, O Glorious and Blessed Virgin.

V. Ora pro nobis, Sancta Dei Genetrix.

V. Pray for us, O Holy Mother of God.

R. Ut digni efficiamur promissionibus Christi. Amen.

R. That we may be made worthy of the promises of Christ. Amen.

Ad mentem Romani Pontificis precamur ut omnes indulgentias Sanctissimo Beatae Mariae Virginis Rosario concessas consequamur: **Pater Noster, Ave Maria, Gloria.**

For the intentions of the Roman Pontiff and to gain the indulgences granted to the Most Holy Rosary of the Most Holy Virgin Mary: Pray one **Our Father**, *one* **Hail Marys** y *one* **Glory be**.

Oremus pro fidelibus defunctis

Let us pray for the faithful departed

V. Réquiem æternam dona eis, Dómine.

V. Eternal rest grant unto them, O Lord

R. Et lux perpetua luceat eis.

R. And let perpetual light shine upon them.

V. Requiescant in pace.	V. May they rest in peace.
R. Amen.	R. Amen.
V. Regina Sacratissimi Rosarii	V. Queen of the Most Holy Rosary.
R. Ora pro nobis.	R. Pray for us.
V. Nos, cum prole pia.	V. Mother with your Blessed Son.
R. Benedicat Virgo María.	R. Bless us each and everyone.
V. O María sine labe concepta.	V. O Mary, conceived without sin.
R. Ora pro nobis, qui confugimus ad Te.	R. Pray for us who have recourse to Thee.

Memorare, O piissima Virgo María, non ese auditum a sæculo, quemquam ad tua currentem præsidia, tua implorantem auxilia, tua petentem suffragia, esse derelictum.

Ego tali animatus confidentia, ad te, Virgo Virginum, Máter, curro, ad te venio, coram te gemens peccator assisto.

Noli, Mater Verbi, verba mea despicere; sed audi propitia et exaudi. Amen.

Remember, O most gracious Virgin Mary, that never was it known that anyone who fled to thy protection, implored thy help, or sought thy intercession, was left unaided.

Inspired by this confidence I fly unto thee, O Virgin of virgins, my Mother. To thee do I come, before thee I stand, sinful and sorrowful.

O Mother of the Word Incarnate, despise not my petitions, but in thy mercy hear and answer me. Amen.

Sancte Míchael Archángele, defénde nos in prœlio: contra nequítiam et insídias diáboli esto præsídium.

Impéret illi Deus, súpplices deprecámur; tuque, Princeps milítiæ cæléstis, Sátanam aliósque spíritus malígnos, qui ad perditiónem animárum pervagántur in mundo, divína virtúte in inférnum detrúde. Amen.

In nomine Patris (†), et Filii, et Spiritus Sancti. Amen.

St. Michael the Archangel, defend us in battle; be our defense against the wickedness and snares of the devil.

May God rebuke him, we humbly pray; and do thou, O Prince of the heavenly host, by the power of God, thrust into hell Satan, and the other evil spirits, who prowl about the world seeking the ruin of souls. Amen.

In the name of the Father (†), and of the Son, and of the Holy Spirit. Amen.

DEO GRATIAS.

Printed in Great Britain
by Amazon